Richard Clarke Cabot

Preliminary note on the prognosis of nephritis

Richard Clarke Cabot

Preliminary note on the prognosis of nephritis

ISBN/EAN: 9783337866495

Printed in Europe, USA, Canada, Australia, Japan

Cover: Foto ©ninafisch / pixelio.de

More available books at **www.hansebooks.com**

PRELIMINARY NOTE ON THE PROGNOSIS OF NEPHRITIS.

By RICHARD C. CABOT, M.D.,

AND

FRANKLIN W. WHITE, M.D.

OF BOSTON.

Read at the Annual Meeting of the Massachusetts Medical Society,
June 13, 1899.

PRELIMINARY NOTE ON THE PROG-
NOSIS OF NEPHRITIS.

THE material upon which this study is based was obtained
as follows : From the records of the Mass. General Hospital
for the last twenty years, the course and symptoms of all
fatal cases of nephritis were noted, and the duration of each
case, from the time of the first symptom to death, was esti-
mated as accurately as possible. In addition to this, circulars
were sent to the address of every patient who had left the
Hospital between 1880 and the present day suffering from
nephritis of any type. By means of these circulars, we
attempted to find out the condition of the patients since
leaving the Hospital, and the date of death in the fatal cases.
Only a portion of those to whom circulars were sent returned
any answer, but the answers received were very instructive.
All of the cases, diagnosed in the Hospital records as nephritis, who returned any answer to our inquiries, were
followed up as carefully as possible, and in many cases the
urine was examined. The number of these cases, together
with the fatal ones, is 332.

In addition to these, we have a considerable body of data,
sent us with great kindness, by a large number of physicians
to whom we wrote, asking whether they had ever known a
case of chronic nephritis to recover, and also how long they
had ever known a case of nephritis to last. This data fur-
nished us details of 91 more cases, making a total of 423 in
all.

We were stimulated to make the above investigations by
the indefiniteness and disagreement of the statements in the

text books on the subject of The Prognosis of Nephritis, especially in its chronic form. Many writers show a strong tendency to hedge when it comes to the question : "Does a case of chronic nephritis, properly certified as such, ever recover?" Thus, for example, Rotch in his Diseases of Children, says of the prognosis of chronic nephritis : "Some cases, having the clinical features of the disease, have apparently recovered." Delafield, in the American System of Medicine, says, under Chronic Diffuse Nephritis, "Recovery seems to be possible." Osler says that in chronic parenchymatous nephritis recovery rarely takes place in a case that has persisted for more than a year, but occasionally, in children, even when the disease has persisted for two years, symptoms disappear and recovery takes place. Senator,* speaking of chronic diffuse nephritis, says that termination in recovery is a rare exception, but undoubtedly occurs. He agrees with Rosenstein that these are usually cases, which after acute onset as a result of infectious disease or exposure, become chronic, and after one and one-half or two years, end in recovery, the urine becoming entirely normal. An entire "restitutio ad integrum" of all the kidney tissue does not occur, but this is not indispensable for complete functional recovery. He also says that death is invariably the result in interstitial nephritis where the typical contracted kidney is developed, and the heart hypertrophy is marked. Recovery (functional) is possible, and under proper treatment is not rare in the first stage, that is, as long as no sign of heart or vessel lesion has developed.

Strümpell, in his last German edition, speaking of chronic diffuse nephritis, says that complete recovery undoubtedly occurs, but is rare. By the passage of the large kidney into secondary contraction "apparent healing" may occur, in which the subjective condition of the patient is almost en-

* Senator, Erkrankungen der Nieren.

tirely satisfactory. He considers chronic interstitial nephritis incurable, though life may be prolonged without any considerable unpleasant symptoms for many years. Bartels, in Zeimssens' Encyclopædia, says that chronic nephritis is incurable after a certain time, but that cases have recovered even after months of dropsy. On the other hand, Brault, in the Traité de Medicine, says that in chronic nephritis the future is always sombre, sooner or later uræmia or a complication leads to a fatal ending. Tyson also, and Loomis, in the Twentieth Century Practice of Medicine, say that cases never recover. In Albutt's System and in Fagge, no definite statements are made on this point.

Under these circumstances, with such variety in the opinions of the foremost writers, our interest centred about the question: " Does a case of chronic nephritis, certified as such, ever recover?"

At this point, it seems best to define what we mean by chronic nephritis and by recovery.

(1) We recognize two important types of chronic nephritis: *(a)* Chronic diffuse nephritis, and *(b)* Chronic interstitial nephritis.

(a) By chronic diffuse nephritis, we mean a disease characterized by prolonged anasarca and effusions into the serous cavities, early and pronounced manifestation of uræmia, such as headache, vomiting and dyspnœa, vascular changes such as cardiac hypertrophy and a high tension pulse, and a pale urine usually diminished in amount, containing a large amount of albumen, with an abundance of fatty elements in the sediment.

(b) By chronic interstitial nephritis, we mean a disease of insidious onset and long course, with comparatively early appearance of the vascular changes above mentioned, and little or no œdema until the heart fails, with late and usually less marked uræmic symptoms, a large amount of urine, of low specific gravity, with albumen present in very small

quantities if at all, and a sediment containing usually only a few hyaline and granular casts.

(2) We consider a patient to have recovered when he has no subjective symptoms characteristic of nephritis, and passes normal urine.

Defining our terms in this way, we come now to the analysis of our cases, and taking first the data from the Massachusetts General Hospital records, we find that of the total 304 cases, in which a diagnosis of chronic nephritis stands recorded on the books or the hospital, and which we have been able to follow up till death, or till the present time, there are only 17 whose urine and general condition show that the patient has really recovered. In most of these cases, although the diagnosis of chronic nephritis stands upon the books, it is difficult to see why it should have been made. From the facts recorded, it was evident, in most of the cases, that the patient was rapidly improving, that the symptoms were of comparatively brief duration, and the diagnosis seemed unjustified. In a few cases, on the other hand, the long duration of the symptoms and the character of the urine indicate an undoubted chronic nephritis followed by a genuine recovery. The following two cases are among the more remarkable of our series.

Case 1.—Woman, age 23. Eight years ago symptoms of chronic diffuse nephritis lasting for two and one-half years, headache, vomiting, marked œdema of body, face and legs, also ascites, which was tapped twice. Urine contained $\frac{1}{4}$ to 1% albumen, and many hyaline, granular and fatty casts. For the last six years she has been perfectly well and leading an active life. The urine examined a year ago and also this year was normal, free from casts and albumen.

Case 2.—Boy, aged 16 years. Chronic diffuse nephritis followed scarlet fever at the age of eight years, lasting for four and one-half years, with headache, vomiting and anasarca. The urine contained $\frac{1}{8}\%$ albumin and many hyaline, granular and epithelial casts. He had several severe exacerbations. Has been perfectly well for three and one-half years, and is now at work. The urine at the present time is perfectly normal.

In answer to the question, " Have you ever known a case of chronic nephritis to recover?" 48 of the physicians who were asked said no, and 21 (about one-third of the whole number) said yes.

Among these latter answers are the following:

(1) Dr. J. M. Da Costa, of Philadelphia, writes of the case of "a young woman, eighteen years of age, who had chronic parenchymatous nephritis of about a year's duration. The disease came on gradually, though there was a statement of its having followed exposure. Dropsy was a marked symptom. There was considerable albumin in the urine, and epithelial casts. She gradually recovered entirely, got married, and became the mother of five children. She was seen last year, and her urine was found to be perfectly normal."

" In a second case, twenty years of age, seen in consultation, the disease of the kidney followed scarlet fever at the age of eight. As a boy, the patient learned to test his urine for albumin, and continued to test it until he was grown up, with the result of never finding albumin absent, though not present in any great quantity. He tested for it and found it only a few months before an exacerbation of the disease, coming on after exposure; in this the urine contained large amounts of albumin and tube casts. Under a rigid milk diet for three months, mild diuretic waters, iron, and other means, the dropsy disappeared, and his general condition greatly improved, but albumin remained. Pursuing treatment for two months more, the albumin gradually disappeared, and, though constantly tested for it (and he was no longer on a restricted diet), none was found for some months afterward, when he was looked upon as having entirely recovered. I never heard of a return of the disease."

"In a third case, a man sixty years of age, who was dropsical for months, there was a history of the kidney disease having begun after exposure about two months before he came under observation. The urine was markedly albuminous and contained tube casts, but no blood casts or blood. Under treatment for ten weeks, the albumin was reduced to a trace, and for some little time was absent; but, a few months afterward, during a period of great family distress, it was again found in the urine, though not in large amount. Under treatment, it slowly disappeared, and, examining him three years afterward, not a trace of kidney disease could be detected. The patient subsequently died of phthisis, which was hereditary in his family."

(2) From Dr. Charles G. Stockton, of Buffalo, we received the following case:

"The case came under my observation in the autumn of 1890. The patient was a woman about 46 years old, of medium height, and weighed about 240 lbs. The exact weight could not be ascertained. She had been in poor health for several years, and for the past six months had suffered from headache, dizziness, anorexia, mental confusion, irregularity of the bowels and increasing general anasarca. The aortic second sound was relatively intense and high pitched; the apex too far to the left, not palpable owing to the fat. There were no bruits. There was an increased arterial tension.

The first recorded examination showed about 12% albumin (by bulk), with hyaline, granular and epithelial casts. A more complete examination was made a few days later when she voided, in 24 hours, 26 ounces of urine containing 27.4 gr. of urea, and albumin about 4%.

Examinations were now made daily, and it was found that the amount of albumin, by Esbach's method, was from two to four grams per litre. The casts continued; sometimes the hyaline form predominated, at other times both finely and coarsely granular casts predominated, and occasionally large numbers of epithelial casts were seen. Under treatment on the 9th of January, 1891, only ½ gram of albumin to the litre was found, and 1,136 c.c. of urine were passed in 24 hours, and the urea had risen to 30.67 grams. This amount did not continue, and she had a number of relapses, judging from the condition of the urine. For instance, on the 14th of January, there was in 1,408 c.c. of urine two grams of albumin per litre ; and the same casts. On the 25th of January, the urine had fallen to 768 c.c., 21 grams of urea, two and one-half grams of albumin per litre ; no casts were found. On February 27th, albumin four grams per litre, urea 29.23 grams, a number of uric acid crystals, hyaline and epithelial casts and renal epithelium. On the 8th of March, the urea had fallen to 19 grams, albumin had risen to 4.50 grams per litre ; there were no hyaline casts. On the 15th of March there were no casts found. Urinary examinations showed varying results, but on the whole about the same for some months therefrom.

In September, there were six grams of albumin to the litre, 832 c.c. of urine, 21 grams of urea ; no casts found. On the 11th of November, a few casts, urea had fallen to 16 grams. From this time on the casts decreased in number and were almost altogether hyaline ; albumin varied. On November 19th, there were five and one-half grams per litre ; December 12th, a few casts. January 3d, 1892, urine 28 ounces, urea 22.4 grams, hyaline, slightly granular casts. July 12th, 1892, ¾ gram of albumin per litre, urea 22 grams, pus corpuscles, epithelium and a few granular casts. December 6th, 1892, more than two years after I first saw her, the albumin was .25 gram per litre, one small granular cast. May 9th, 1893, there was no albumin, urea 23.71 and no casts found. From this time on the urea was less in amount, the urine became more abundant; albumin was found in varying quantities, usually in traces only, and occasionally hyaline and slightly granular casts. For the past three years I have found that the urine has been uniformally free from albumin and casts. The patient's general condition corresponded rather closely with the state of her urine. Her symptoms were somewhat promptly relieved by treatment, but there was more or less edema for at least a year after I first saw her. Her vision was disturbed in the beginning, but an eye examination showed that the retina was not affected. I have a report on the condition of the retina reaching back as far as 1888."

(3) From Dr. D. W. Prentiss, of Washington, the following note:

"A case of chronic parenchymatous nephritis, had been ill about six months when I first saw him. Diagnosis unmistakable. Recovered in about a year. This was 18 years ago. He is still well, and has been working at his trade ever since. Theory of recovery: that but one kidney was affected."

(4) From Dr. G. Baumgarten, of St. Louis, the following:

"In August, 1894, the patient had edema of the face and hands. In October, 1894, extensive anasarca was present; urine about normal in quantity, 1,015, 1½–2% of albumin, granular casts, leucocytes, no blood. December 25, 1894, much better; anasarca about the same, urine 1½% albumin, many casts. January, 1899, dropsy began to disappear; returned to work. May, 1896, feels well; urine 1,029, with a trace of albumin and few casts. April, 1897, excellent health; urine free from albumin and casts; has remained well to this day."

Other physicians who have known cases of chronic nephritis to recover are H. C. Wood and J. P. C. Griffith of

Philadelphia; Beverley Robinson, J. S. Billings and G. L. Peabody of New York; J. B. Herrick of Chicago; E. L. Trudeau of Saranac; and W. S. Thayer of Baltimore.

"LATENT" CASES.

In addition to our recovered cases there are nine patients who are at work and in good health at the present time, despite the presence of albumin and casts in greater or less quantity in the urine. The duration of these cases, from the first symptoms suggestive of nephritis up to the present time, is as follows:

1 for 6 months.	1 for 10 years.
2 " 5 years.	1 " 11 "
1 " 7 "	1 " 12 "
2 " 8 "	

Many of these "latent cases" were very striking. The people were able to work hard and steadily for years at a time without interruption, and were entirely free from any disagreeable signs or symptoms, while at the same time the urine contained from a trace to $\frac{1}{4}\%$ of albumin and an abundance of casts.

Among the "latent" cases of which notes were sent us by other physicians are the following:

Dr. Franz Pfaff, of Boston, has under observation a patient who has had nephritis for 25 years. The urine shows, as the result of repeated examinations, the following characteristics: amount, 1,680 cu. c.m.; specific gravity, 1,009; albumin very large trace; urea, 1.13%; hundreds of casts in large slide, hyaline, fine granular, coarse granular, a few very highly refracting. Many of the casts are fatty and have renal cells adherent.

Dr. Wharton Sinkler, of Philadelphia, sends the following cases:

No. 1. Mrs. W. had puerperal nephritis and lived 25 years with it. The urine always contained albumin.

No. 2.   Mr. E. has had nephritis for about 20 years. It began with an acute attack, with bloody urine.   He is still in fair health, though the urine contains albumin.

Dr. Isaac Alder, of New York, sends the following :

"I have under observation a case of chronic parenchymatous nephritis which had lasted for 26 years, and still shows but little disturbances of general health ; no edema ; no ascites.   The urine contains, on the average, two per mille of albumin (Esbach) with granular and fatty casts."

Dr. Alfred Stengel, of Philadelphia, says : "I have under my care two physicians.   One has had albumin, casts, and the general symptoms suggestive of chronic interstitial nephritis for ten years to my knowledge.   He himself believes that he has had it for 20 years, having discovered albumin in his urine as long ago as that."

"Another case which occurs to me is a lady who has had nephritis certainly for twelve years.   Lately, there has been a little swelling of the feet, but this is the only symptom I have ever discovered suggestive of nephritis."

Dr. James Tyson, of Philadelphia, writes :

"Recently I was asked for an opinion in the case of an army officer who had an acknowledged uræmic convulsion 29 years ago ; returned to duty, and remained on duty until last summer, when he died of Bright's disease."

AVERAGE DURATION.

Two hundred and sixty-nine of our cases have died. *The average duration of these fatal cases from start to finish was 19 months.* 40 of our cases lasted less than two months from the first symptom to the time of death.   152 cases lasted two months to two years, and 46 cases from two to five years. The seven longest cases in our series lived 7, 10, 12, 14, 16, 20 and 23 years respectively. Of the fatal cases, 210 were of the type of chronic diffuse nephritis (under which we include those ordinarily classed as chronic parenchymatous nephritis), and 52 were of the interstitial type.

In the list of 91 cases of long duration sent us by physicians 27 had lasted from 10 to 15 years,

    16   "   "   "   15 to 20   "
     6   "   "   over 20 years, namely, 1 for 22 years.
                                3 " 25   "
                                1 " 28   "
                                1 " 30   "

The number of acute cases in our series was so small that it seemed best to discard them. It is a notable fact, in this connection, that for the last five years, the number of cases diagnosed as acute nephritis at the Massachusetts General Hospital has steadily diminished. We interpret this to mean that cases formerly called acute are now considered as acute exacerbations of chronic cases.

RELATION BETWEEN ETIOLOGY AND PROGNOSIS.

The nine cases in which there was a distinct history of lead poisoning ran a comparatively long course. The same is true of the 16 cases in which syphilis occurred. Some of the shortest cases, if we are to judge simply by the duration of definite symptoms, were those associated with arteriosclerosis, in which fatal uræmia came on out of a clear sky and killed a patient within a week.

Curiously enough the 57 cases in which the only possible etiological factor obtainable was heredity, that is, a family history of nephritis, "dropsy," apoplexy, heart disease or phthisis, seemed to run a relatively long course.

We were unable to observe any relation between the duration of cases and the occurrence of such etiological factors as abuse of alcohol, infectious diseases, pregnancy, or exposure to cold. *In the vast majority of our cases no cause of any kind could be traced.*

EFFECT OF COMPLICATIONS UPON PROGNOSIS.

Complications were the cause of death (apparently) in 44 cases out of our 332. Pneumonia and pericarditis were the most frequent complications, and phthisis next. Pneumonia and pericarditis have occurred with about equal frequency, and our statistics indicate that pneumonia is equally common as a cause of death in cases of short and of long duration, while pericarditis seems more apt to carry off a patient at a comparatively early stage of the disease. Thus of the 11 cases ending fatally with acute pneumonia, five cases had a duration of less than two years, and six cases of two years or more. On the other hand, only two of the 15 cases ending with acute pericarditis had a duration of two or more years.

As cases of nephritis get on past the first year the dangers of such complications as cerebral haemorrhage, hemiplegia and gangrene increase.

RELATION OF DROPSY TO PROGNOSIS.

It has been said by good authorities that the prognosis in diffuse nephritis is worse in cases where dropsy is marked, but in 47 cases of our series, in which no dropsy occurred, the average duration was 10 months, compared to 23 months, which is the average duration of the cases in which dropsy *was* present. In short, the course of the disease in the cases of diffuse nephritis without dropsy was less than half as long as in the cases with dropsy.

Dropsy is not sufficiently common in interstitial nephritis to be of much prognostic value.

RELATION OF RETINAL CHANGES TO PROGNOSIS.

Good authorities state that cases of chronic nephritis rarely last more than two years after the presence of haemorrhages in the retina. This is borne out by our series of cases, of which only one lived over two years from the time at which haemorrhages were seen in the fundus oculi. In this case, however, the patient lived five years and seven months after the date at which retinal hæmorrhages in both eyes were observed by Dr. Wadsworth at the Massachusetts General Hospital.

CARDIAC ENLARGEMENT AND PROGNOSIS.

Occurrence of hypertrophy of the heart is universally acknowledged as marking the advance of the disease beyond the curable stage. This is borne out by our statistics of the 104 cases in which cardiac enlargement was demonstrated. Only three lived more than two years from the date at which the enlargement was demonstrated.

CONCLUSIONS.

We will summarize our results as follows :

1. Chronic nephritis is not an absolutely incurable disease. Recovery occurs in rare instances.

2. Chronic nephritis may exist for a long series of years without causing any apparent constitutional disturbance.

3. The average duration in 332 cases of chronic nephritis was nineteen months.

4. Acute nephritis is less common than has been supposed, many cases formerly diagnosed as such have been shown to represent exacerbations in chronic nephritis.